UNKNOWN

Unknown
a play

**by
Alexis Clements**

Private Commision
Brooklyn, NY

Published by
Private Commission
Brooklyn, NY

© 2014 Alexis Clements, Revised Edition

All rights reserved. No part of this publication may be reproduced or transmitted in any form or by any means, electronic or otherwise, without written permission from Alexis Clements.

CAUTION: This play is fully protected, in part or in any form, under United States of America as well as International copyright laws and is subject to royalty. All rights, including professional, amateur, motion picture, radio, television, recitation, public reading, and any method of photographic reproduction are strictly reserved. All inquiries concerning amateur and stock performances should be addressed to Alexis Clements (www.alexisclements.com).

ISBN 978-0-578-15275-2

Printed in the United States of America

To those who remain unknown to me but whose words have given me solace, strength, and offered challenges.

Contents

About the Play	xi
Unknown	3
Acknowledgements	81
About the Author	83
Colophon	84

About the Play

When I began writing this play I had been volunteering on and off, on a very casual basis, at the Lesbian Herstory Archives in Brooklyn, NY. I still didn't know many of the people there and often kept largely to myself. But the place itself fascinated me and also provided a setting in which to bounce ideas of myself off of others, past and present. The extremely idiosyncratic nature of the collection and its organization ran counter to the highly ordered and largely hierarchical nature of pretty much every collection of things I had encountered in institutional settings up to that point. I came to love the orderly disorder that I perceived within the Archives, as it allowed for many unexpected discoveries and encounters, and it defied many assumptions and expectations.

A couple of months after starting some early sketches of the play I decided to enroll in a class being offered for the first time at the Archives—"Lesbian Lives." Taught by the art historian, writer, activist, and artist Flavia Rando, the course offered a space for conversation among a group of women spanning at least three generations. It was through that course that I began to get to know the Archives and all that it represents much better.

The Lesbian Herstory Archives is celebrating its 40th year as I type this. Founded in 1974, it grew out of a female-focused consciousness-raising group that formed following a conference held by the Gay Academic Union in New York City. From discussions within that group, a larger project was launched to create a "grassroots Lesbian archive." For the first 15 years of its existence it was housed in part of the Manhattan apartment of two of its founders, Deb Edel and Joan Nestle. In the 1980s, members of the collective began a campaign to raise money for the purchase of a home specifically for the Archives, eventually gathering enough to purchase a brownstone in the Park Slope neighborhood of Brooklyn, where the Archives remains today.

The Lesbian Lives class, taught within the main reading room of the Archives' Brooklyn home, was originally planned for only the fall of 2011, but because none of us wanted to stop, it extended into the spring of 2012. Since then, a number of us have gathered and formed friendships lasting well beyond the class itself.

As our class ended in spring of 2012, each of us presented a project that referenced the Archives' collection in some way. Since I had recently finished a draft of the play I was ready to share, I decided to present that. But rather than bring in a director and actors or partner with a theater, as is often typical for first public readings of plays, I decided instead to ask those who came to the event to read the play aloud. And so, on a cool evening in April, we readers, sitting in front of our audience, formed a tight little semicircle on a hodge podge of chairs and the well-used purple sofa that anchors the Archives' reading room. Deb Edel, one of the Archives' founders read the role of Sydney, and a couple of people from the Lesbian Lives class took other roles, with volunteers from the audience filling out the cast.

The experience of sharing this play in that particular way is what gave rise to a larger project that I continue to work on at this moment. The Unknown Play Project, as it's currently called, combines community-based readings of *Unknown*, with a documentary film examining changes happening within many lesbian and queer women's spaces, and an interactive art installation (still in development) that will form its own archive of sorts. To learn more about that project, visit www.unknownplayproject.org.

Please note that the people in this play are not depictions of specific people from the Archives' community. They are an amalgam of impressions, ideas, imaginings, and chance encounters from across my lifetime. They represent the questions, love, and sense of community that I personally experienced in that space. They also touch on some of the conflicts and contradictions that I feel in that space as well as others. But they do not represent a summary or complete description of what the Archives itself is—that would be an impossible project. The only way to get a sense of the real place is to visit.

Unknown

Characters (in order of appearance)
Sydney Anders (née Isabella Ricci), 87 years old, an Italian-American woman.
Sophie, 30 years old, a white woman.
Thea, 15 years old, a young African American woman.
Popcorn (real name Nikki), 35 years old, an African American woman.
Volunteer, a woman (possibly doubled with Beverly or Imari).
Imari, 29 years old, a mixed-race (Asian and Latina heritage) woman.
Beverly Longie, 62 years old, a Native American woman (Dakota), a social worker.

Setting
An old brownstone in Brooklyn, NY, that was converted into an archive thirty-five years ago. The set should contain the following: a front door, a main reading room, a workroom with a computer and a large table, and a small kitchen.

Sydney's home should be superimposed on the Archives—in other words, the same set should be used for both spaces, with lighting or projections used to differentiate them.

The set should not be realistic or naturalistic. In other words it should not try to literally recreate the Archives. There should be a focus on categories, types, or archetypes in the design, rather than on specific objects. And the scale—too tall, too wide, too something—should help emphasize the fact that there is both too much and not enough to be contained in the space—that categories change and are revised or shift too often to keep up.

There needs to be at least one surface for projecting on the set.

Note
There are some scenes that include or are made up entirely of projections and recordings of Sydney's voice. These are denoted in the script by the sections marked **Projection**.

UNKNOWN

Opening

Stagehand enters the stage and turns on a reel-to-reel recorder. Then she exits.

Sydney (*Recorded.*) I am invisible. They don't see me. They never did. Even then; even when I was a cute little girl on the arm of the town's favorite son—curly-haired and smiling; rosy cheeks and a ripe bottom that Daniel liked to pat. But I was just another one of them, another sweet-faced girl, another young thing that would eventually turn into something else—a wife, a mother, a widow, a soft old lady, an object to tuck away in a box, to take out and touch and reminisce over occasionally, just for a little while. But then after everything happened, after they, for the first time, looked long and hard at me, they closed their eyes completely. They never wanted to look at me again. It didn't matter what I would become. I was erased. And I let them erase me. I helped them. I moved away. I changed my name. I left and never came back, never even tried to make contact. I made sure I would never disturb their vision again.

We hear the sound of fingers running over the spines of books on a shelf. Lights up on Thea, who is tracing her fingers over the shelves and shelves of books in the main room of the Archives. The sound continues as she continues, moving from shelf to shelf, bookcase to bookcase.

Sophie is also on the stage, opening mail at the large old wooden table in the work room.

Sydney (*Recorded.*) It's hard to remember exactly how it happened. By the time it started it was already too late to stop it. I was so young, I didn't know anything about the world. How could I? They hemmed us in so much—there were only certain sorts of things they wanted us to see. I don't know where she learned the things she learned. She must have read about them in books or magazines. Just the idea that it was even possible to love another woman… (*Beat.*) When it happened, when her father came in to the shop and found us there kissing, he pulled me back and beat me square on the jaw. I thought he was going to kill me. I assumed my life would end right there on that floor. But he held himself off from hitting me again. He picked me up and pushed me out the door, told me he would come after me with a gun if he ever saw me again. He probably guessed what I already knew—that he didn't have to kill me because my father would do it when he found out.

Thea walks back to where Sophie is working and starts looking through some of the papers and photographs laying on the table.

Thea (*Holding a photograph in her hand.*) Which one do you think is the lesbian—the little girl or her mother?

Sophie (*Trying to get some work done.*) How do you know that's her mother?

Thea Why else would she be in the picture?

Sophie It could be her aunt or a friend. Or she could be adopted.

Thea Even if she was adopted, it would still be her mom.

Sophie Sorry, Thea, you're right, that was a careless thing to say.

Thea helps Sophie with opening the mail.

Sydney (*Recorded.*) I thought that being alone would allow me to let go, to feel a sense of release. Like taking off your clothes before a shower—letting them fall on the floor and leaving them there while you step under the water.

Lights fade out.

Scene 1

Sophie carries a heavy box in from the front stoop. She walks back out for another, carrying that one in as well. As she brings the second one in to place it on the table, Thea enters.

Thea What's in the boxes?

Sophie I don't know yet.

Thea Want some help?

Sophie They're heavy. I don't want you to get hurt.

Sophie turns to get another one.

Thea You think you're stronger than me?

Sophie No, I just don't want you to get hurt.

Thea But you're okay with hurting yourself?

Sophie carries a new box in.

Thea Give me that.

Thea takes the box from Sophie, while Sophie retrieves another.

Thea Where is everybody?

Sophie It's still early. And it's a nice day out. It'll probably be quiet today.

Sophie and Thea carry in the last two boxes.

Thea Any volunteers coming?

Sophie I'm a volunteer.

Thea You know what I mean.

Sophie I don't think so. There weren't any notes on the calendar.

Thea Is that how you know who's coming?

They each place a box on the table.

Sophie Only if they tell someone they're coming. Most of them just drop in. Like you.

Thea But I'm not a volunteer.

Sophie You're carrying boxes.

Thea I'm doing research.

Sophie Oh yeah, into what?

Thea Everything.

Sophie The whole universe?

Thea Everything that's here.

Sophie I should get you to update the catalogue while you're at it. Or have you re-shelve the books—everything is always completely out of order.

Thea I don't want to work. My parents say I need to take a break. That's why I come here.

Sophie In that case, you should be out in the park on a bicycle. Or walking through the city, exploring—not in here.

Thea Why? You don't like me?

Sophie I just mean you should be getting some fresh air.

Thea I'm not a kid. I stopped growing like six years ago. I don't need any more fresh air.

Sophie Okay.

Sophie sits down at the computer and starts to work.

Thea (*Referring to the boxes.*) You're not going to open these?

Sophie Not right now. I've got a bunch of other things to do. If I open them now I'm going to have to go through everything and I don't think I have time for that today?

Thea You leaving early?

Sophie Yeah.

Thea Who's taking over?

Sophie Popcorn said she would come down.

Thea I hate Popcorn.

Sophie You should really figure out a way to get over that. She's a great lady.

Thea She hates me.

Sophie I doubt it.

Thea She does, I know it. She always gives me this really nasty look every time she sees me, like she thinks I shouldn't be allowed in here.

Sophie Thea, I'm sorry, but I'm gonna need to focus on this for a bit, okay?

Thea Sure. Whatever.

Sophie I've just got a lot to sort through.

Thea Yeah, okay. I'll be in the other room.

Thea sulks off into the main room. She runs her fingers along the shelves for a little while and then she pulls a book down and curls up on the couch with it.

Scene 2

Popcorn is giving a Volunteer a brief tour.

Popcorn The collection is more than just books. We also have photographs, t-shirts, protest banners, films, recordings. There's storage in the basement and off-site. Upstairs is mostly journals and a few of the special collections. Almost everything here has been donated. We don't really have a budget for acquisition, most of the money goes into maintenance and upkeep. The catalogues are all on the computer now, but they're a mixed bag. Some people knew what they were doing when they made them and others didn't, so we're always working on updating those. Plus, there are a lot of differing opinions about how things should be catalogued—what categories to use, that kind of thing.

Projection

We see Sydney's hands writing into a large journal, the sound of the pen on the paper is audible.

Popcorn (*We hear only her voice.*) We also take personal collections, from anyone—they don't have to be famous. The whole point is to create a collection that gives a complete picture—not just of a certain kind of lesbian, but the entire spectrum, from every class, ethnicity, race, religion.

Scene 3

The projection of Sydney writing continues, but moves to a small screen, perhaps a television screen, and continues throughout this scene.

Sophie is working at the computer again. There is a Volunteer going through a number of papers on the table.

Volunteer How should I file these?

Sophie You have to go by first name if it's a person, then there are subject files if there's no name attached. The subject file hasn't been updated in a long time, but you can kind of flip through and you'll start to see how it works.

Volunteer Why first name?

Sophie The last name is a surname, given by the father.

Volunteer I don't get it.

Sophie You have to understand, the women who founded this place were Radicalesbians. The whole point was to have women's stories told without the imposition of a male, heterosexual society.

Volunteer Hmmm.

Both go back to their work for a time.

Volunteer So, how do people search through all this stuff? I mean, it seems a little confusing to me.

Sophie You get used to it quick. You just have to think a little differently than you've been trained. Plus, we have a catalogue. It's a little outdated at this point, we're trying to update it.

Volunteer It just seems a little hard to figure out what's here. Like in these files, some of the things in these folders seem a little arbitrary.

Sophie I guess that's a metaphor for life, isn't it?

Volunteer Huh?

Scene 4

Sophie is standing, facing the audience, as if they are a crowd of people gathered in the Archive.

Sophie Those of you who live in the neighborhood have likely walked by here without even realizing we're here. From the outside it looks like an ordinary brownstone. The women who founded it wanted it to be a safe place for women to come and find resources they couldn't find anywhere else, to read stories they had never been able to read before, and to share their experiences. But to some the way it blends in makes them think about the way that we have been invisible in the culture for so long, the way others have tried to wipe us out of history, or misname us. (*Beat.*) I guess it's like everything else—it's hard to strike the right balance. But then again, everyone is always asking women to figure out how to balance everything. Maybe that's not really the point.

Scene 5

Sophie hands Thea a box cutter. They are both standing around the large table where the boxes they brought in earlier are sitting.

Thea Are you sure you trust me?

Sophie It should just be a bunch of books and papers, it's not like there's hidden treasure in there. Just don't go crazy with the box cutter.

Thea But I thought you people thought this stuff was hidden treasure.

Sophie (*Pointing to one of the boxes.*) Let's start with this one.

Thea carefully cuts open the box Sophie indicated. They both pull the top open to see what's inside. Thea pulls out one of the journals.

Thea They're all old diaries. (*Beat.*) You think there's anything good in them?

Sophie looks through the box. She pulls out a sheet of paper.

Sophie This is a really old acquisition form. I don't think they've used these for years.

Thea What's her name?

Sophie reads through the paper.

Sophie Sydney Anders. Six boxes of personal journals and recordings, and a selection of poetry.

Thea Was she famous?

Sophie I've never heard of her, but that doesn't matter.

Beat.

Thea (*Flipping through one of the diaries.*) I would never let anyone read my diaries, even if I was dead.

Sophie You're only fifteen. You might think differently about it when you get older.

Thea Hell no, I won't. That stuff is private. No one will ever read it.

Sophie Let me have the box cutter.

Thea I'll do it.

Thea cuts open the other boxes and Sophie goes through the contents.

Thea We should Google her, see who she was.

Sophie Who she was is right here in front of us.

Thea You know what I mean.

Sophie We want every woman's story.

Thea No you don't.

Sophie Yes, we do.

Thea What about that lady in here the other day who wouldn't shut up about her swollen ankles?

Sophie If she wanted to send her papers in, we would take them.

Thea But she's boring and unhappy.

Sophie You don't know that, Thea.

Thea Whatever.

Sophie starts pulling papers out of the boxes and looks through the cassette tapes and recordings. Then she goes to retrieve some papers from the desk and sits down to start filling them out.

Meanwhile, Thea picks out a new journal and starts reading it aloud.

Thea "The thrashers are making a nest in the bramble near the drive. They've taken some of the hay I brought in for the garden. I imagine they'll have it finished by the end of the week." (*Beat.*) What is she—the dyke Martha Stewart or something? (*Sophie keeps working. Thea flips further through the diary looking for something good.*) "I dreamt of Gio last night." Do you think that's a lover?

Sophie Sounds like a man's name.

Thea "We were both at the beach, sitting and talking. He was still the same age…" Too bad, it is a dude.

Sophie Keep reading.

Thea "He was still the same age, but I was my age now. Forty years later." This is boring.

Sophie Do you think he died?

Thea "I was asking him about mother. If he thought she ever knew about him." (*Beat.*) Who cares about dreams anyway?

Sophie Keep going.

Thea "He said he wished she didn't know. He wished he hadn't known. Then he could have just gone along and lived his life the way they would have wanted. I didn't believe him. I told him so, but he started to cry. Then I woke up. His spirit stayed with me all day." (*Beat.*) She's one of these airy-fairy ladies—spirits and auras and voodoo and shit.

Sophie My mother believes in all that stuff.

Thea Really?

Sophie Yeah, she was a total hippy.

Thea Did she do a lot of drugs?

Sophie Yeah.

Thea Did she tell you about it?

Sophie A little bit.

Thea Have you ever tried any drugs?

Sophie I tried a few, but I didn't really like them that much.

Thea Why not? Weren't they any fun?

Sophie Sometimes, but there are parts that aren't fun.

Thea You're just saying that because you want to set some kind of example for me.

Sophie No, I'm saying it because it's true. I wasn't thinking about you.

Thea What did you try?

Sophie I don't think we should keep going with this conversation, Thea. This is stuff you should be talking about with your parents.

Thea Why? They don't tell me the truth about anything and they don't want to hear it when I tell them the truth. Why should I ever have to talk to them?

Sophie I've got to work on these journals.

Thea You always do that when you don't want to talk to me anymore—"I've got a lot of work to do." I hate it when you do that—it's just like my mother.

Sophie You're welcome to help me, but I do have to get these written up now that we've opened the boxes.

Thea Fine. What do you want me to do?

Sophie Find the very first journal. We'll start from there. We need to mark down the dates that each one covers and then we'll have to figure out what's on those tapes.

Thea pulls out a few of the journals, looking at the dates of each entry, while Sophie writes notes.

Thea Here, I think this is the first one.

Sophie What's the date of the first entry?

Thea March 14, 1943.

Sophie Can I see?

Thea You don't believe me?

Sophie I just want to read it.

Sydney (*Just her voice.*) I've never kept a journal before. I've only ever written in exam books and on scraps of paper. Harriet gave me this diary. She said I should write down everything that comes into my head. That it will keep me from getting lonely or from driving myself crazy in this place. I'm staying at the YWCA in Pittsburgh. It's been five months since I left home. I go by Sydney now, Sydney Anders. Everyone here thinks I'm Greek or Dutch. Maybe I shouldn't be writing these things down. Someone is liable to read them. (*Beat.*) I have a job. One of the ladies who runs the place helped me get a position at the Westinghouse factory. A couple of the other girls work there too. There's loads of work in the factories with the war on. I suppose Miss Royce knows somebody who gets us the jobs. If we can get enough money together a couple of the other girls are talking about getting rooms together somewhere else. I don't know much about it, but I suppose it would be good to have a kitchen and not have Miss Royce looking in on us all the time. (*Beat.*) Today is my birthday. I haven't told anyone. I'm eighteen years old. A year older than my brother Gio now. I miss him.

Scene 6

Sophie is alone, packing up the boxes. Imari walks in, startling Sophie.

Sophie You scared me.

Imari What are you doing?

Sophie Getting ready to go.

Imari You wanna grab a coffee together?

Sophie No, thanks. I gotta get home.

Imari You can't take an hour off?

Sophie No, I've got to finish a paper for school.

Imari You've been working all day.

Sophie We agreed to take a break.

Imari Come on, Sophie. We haven't talked in over a week.

Sophie It's only been a couple days.

Imari Do you always have to be right?

Sophie looks at Imari but says nothing. Imari starts to look into the boxes.

Imari Who are these from?

Sophie I really have a lot to do.

Imari Okay. I got it. I hate it when you say that instead of just saying you want some time to yourself.

Sophie We can talk tomorrow after I'm done with class.

Imari Cool. I could stop and get your favorite salad from Constantine's and bring it over.

Sophie I'd rather we just speak on the phone.

Imari Look, I have few things I want to say to you. (*She touches Sophie.*) I don't want to do it here, I want to do it in private.

Beat.

Sophie I'll call you tomorrow.

Imari My phone might not be working—you know how it is.

Sophie Then you should get it fixed.

Imari What kind of thing is that to say?

Sophie You need to go now.

Imari I'll see you tomorrow. (*She kisses Sophie's cheek.*)

Sophie stands and watches Imari go.

Scene 7

Beverly at Sydney's front door. She knocks.

Beverly Ms Anders? Are you home?

She peers in through the glass beside the door, but sees nothing. She knocks again.

Beverly Ms Anders?

She knocks one more time.

Beverly I just wanted to stop by and say hello. I think we know some of the same people. (*Beat.*) Okay. Well, I'll stop by again some other time.

She waits a couple of beats, listening before leaving.

Scene 8

Thea is sitting at the table reading one of the journals while Sophie is busy processing all of them—emptying each box completely, writing down the information for each item, then laying it out on the table.

Thea Why do you come here so much?

Sophie Why do you?

Thea I asked first.

Sophie Because I like it here.

Thea But why?

Sophie It makes me think about my younger self. I think about how much I would have liked to have had a place like this to come to when I was a teenager—to help me figure out who I was. I probably would have been a little like you, hanging out here a lot, reading the books, looking at all the pictures. I couldn't ever find any of these stories when I was younger. I think it would have helped me a lot. This could have been my hiding place.

Thea Is that why you think I come here—to hide?

Sophie I don't know that much about you, Thea. You don't tell me much about yourself.

Thea I come here to get away from the other kids—they're all jerks. My parents think this place is just a library, so they don't care. They think I'm learning or some shit.

Sophie Do they know you're gay?

Thea Who says I'm gay?

Sophie Sorry.

Pause.

Thea Do I look gay?

Sophie Nobody looks gay, Thea. You look like a beautiful young girl.

Thea Really?

Sophie Sure. Don't you think so?

Thea I'm not pretty like you. You probably get asked out all the time.

Sophie That's not really how it works with lesbians.

Thea What do you mean? I bet Imari worked extra hard to get you to go out with her.

Sophie I probably shouldn't talk about my love life with you, Thea.

Thea Why not? That's all anybody ever wants to talk about when they come in here—who's dating who, who's single, what happened in somebody else's relationship.

Sophie I don't tell most people about my love life.

Thea Whatever.

Beat.

Sophie How is school going? How are your parents?

Thea My parents don't understand me. I don't have any close friends, and my teachers hate me.

Sophie No one understands fifteen year olds.

Thea What is that supposed to mean?

Sophie Just that everybody has a hard time at that age.

Thea Yeah, well, I'm not everybody.

Sophie I know.

Thea Do you? Did you know I was adopted? Did you know that my parents are both white? Did you know that they're straight too?

Sophie No, I didn't know that.

Thea Yeah, well, it sucks.

Sophie Do you have anyone you feel like you can talk to about it?

Thea My parents want me to see a shrink, but fuck that. I'm not gonna sit in a room with some white bitch who doesn't know anything about my life.

Sophie Have you tried it?

Thea No. And I'm not going to.

Sophie You might be surprised. I went to a shrink for a couple years and I thought it was really helpful.

Thea Really?

Sophie Yeah. When I was twenty-five and twenty-six. I was just coming out and I was having a hard time with it.

Thea You didn't come out until you were twenty-five?

Sophie Twenty-six, actually.

Thea What took you so long? Was something wrong with you?

Sophie You know, Thea, everybody has their own path. Some people don't come out until much later.

Thea That's lame.

Sophie I don't think you're being very fair.

Thea Who cares? Life isn't fair.

Sophie Do you realize that in some countries it's against the law to be gay? And that some religions think that being gay goes against their beliefs.

Thea I'm not an idiot. I know people are beaten and killed for this, raped, burned, and all that shit. I don't live in a fucking basement somewhere.

Sophie Don't you think that would make it hard for some people to come out?

Thea What made it so hard for you?

Sophie A few things.

Thea Like what?

Beat.

Sophie Well, one thing was a fear that my parents wouldn't love me anymore.

Thea My parents keep trying to tell me they love me no matter what. I mean give me a break. That's bullshit. They hate me. They always have—the way they look at me when I get in trouble, like they want to give me back, like I'm too much to handle, like I'm not what they wanted me to be.

Sophie Do your parents know what kind of Archive this is?

Thea My mother made me show her the website.

Sophie Do you think maybe they're letting you explore this on your own? That they really do love you and want you to be able to figure this out for yourself?

Thea Stop trying to be all therapist-y on me.

Sophie Okay. Maybe we should talk about something else then.

Beat.

Thea Why else did it take you so long?

Beat.

Sophie It's not like there's one specific thing. (*Beat.*) I could give you three or four reasons, but I wouldn't feel certain they were the only ones, or the real ones. I think a big part of it was that I didn't know anyone else like me. No one I knew in school was gay—at least no one was out. And when I tried to talk to people about it they didn't want to talk, they would get uncomfortable and change the subject, or giggle like I was some kind of freak for even saying those words out loud. And at my church they thought being gay was evil. I just remember thinking I was the only one, that there was no one else out there like me, and even in college, when I did meet other lesbians, I was too scared to talk to them, I didn't think I was like them, I didn't think they would let me in—I thought I needed other people to let me into their world.

Thea What about all the fags? I mean you can't turn around in this city without running into one.

Sophie I don't like that word, Thea.

Thea Sorry, the ho-mo-sex-u-al males.

Sophie They were men. They weren't like me. Of course I could see them. Everyone can see them. But I never saw any women, not like me. Or I wouldn't let myself see them. I feel like they were impossible to find when I was younger. Like they were hidden and I didn't know the secret places to find them. It seems ridiculous—it is. But that's what I thought, that's what I told myself.

Thea Where did you grow up?

Sophie North Carolina.

Thea Isn't everybody crazy in the South?

Sophie No, Thea. They aren't. They're no crazier than anywhere else.

Beat.

Thea Can I ask you something?

Sophie Sure.

Thea Why do you always have that pin on your bag?

Sophie The pink one?

Thea Yeah.

Sophie Because I want people to know that I'm gay.

Thea But why? Why do you want everybody to know? Aren't you scared that they might say something to you or do something?

Sophie I don't want to just blend in. I think most people assume I'm straight because I don't fit their stereotype of what lesbians look like. I don't want to just pass.

Thea What do you mean, pass? You're not black.

Sophie It can mean a lot of things for a lot of different people.

Thea I don't think you should use it.

Sophie Okay.

Beat.

Thea I can't pass for anything. No one thinks I'm my parents kid. No one thinks I'm a good student. No one thinks I'm straight. You could be anything you want and no one would care, because you're pretty and you're white.

Sophie All I mean to say is that I want to catch people's assumptions about me, let them know they're wrong, when I can.

Thea Yeah, well, people make assumptions about everybody, all the time. And if you're like me—one of the only black kids in your school, definitely the only one with white parents, and the only one that dresses like a dude, then they don't want anything to do with you. They think you're trouble and that all you're ever gonna be is trouble.

Sophie Sorry, Thea.

Thea What are you apologizing for?

Popcorn walks in with a mug and a bowl.

Popcorn I found these upstairs, Soph.

Sophie Must have been the new volunteer. Sorry. I'll talk to her about it next weekend.

Thea No, "hello," "how are you?"

Popcorn Shouldn't you be doing homework, at home?

Thea That's why I'm here—studying history.

Popcorn Just make sure you keep it down, it's supposed to be quiet here.

Thea Yes, ma'am.

Popcorn Don't pull that shit with me. We're not all gonna treat you like Sophie does.

Thea Who says that/

Sophie Thea!

Thea Yeah, whatever.

Popcorn walks into the kitchen, puts the mug and bowl down and then exits.

Thea (*In a low voice.*) That bitch is never gonna get any love.

Sophie Actually, she's married.

Thea Really?

Sophie Her wife is overseas, working for the State Department.

Thea Whatever.

Beat.

Sophie (*Indicating one of the journals in front of Thea.*) Can you hand me that journal, please?

Thea Here. (*She hands the journal to Sophie.*) I gotta go.

Sophie Just like that?

Thea You've got work to do.

Sophie What about you?

Thea I just remembered something I have to do.

Sophie What's that?

Thea Now you don't want me to leave?

Sophie I just want to make sure it's not because I hurt your feelings.

Thea Yes, Soph. You really hurt me. I think I'm gonna cry now.

Beat.

Sophie When will I see you back here?

Thea I'll be around.

Sophie Okay. (*Beat.*) Well, good-bye.

Thea Later.

Thea exits.

Projection

Sydney's hands, sorting through photographs of herself as a young woman, of other young women, of her brother and her sisters.

Sydney (*Only her voice.*) I gave up on love almost immediately after I figured out what it was. What other choice did I have? After what happened with Margaret in the store that day I knew it would never be worth the risk. I just had to stop thinking about it, stop thinking it was ever going to be something I could have. I just needed to put that part of myself away. (*Beat.*) When Elisabeta brought Henry to me, that was a different kind of love. He wasn't my own, from me, but he was the only thing I'd ever been able to love freely, openly, in any way. I had never planned on being a mother. I never thought of myself that way. And I never really wanted to let him think of me as his mother—it didn't seem like my right. But I think now that if it hadn't been for Henry, I never would have found Ruth.

Scene 9

Imari and Sophie are on the couch at the Archives. Imari is rubbing Sophie's feet.

Imari Come on, baby. You say the same thing every time. It's not fair. You don't really tell me what's going on with you.

Sophie Yes, I do. You just don't listen.

Imari Okay. Then, tell me. What is it? What's going on with you?

Sophie You already know. Grad school is driving me crazy. And then working shifts at the bookstore. And then here, at the Archives. I'm stressed out. And…

Imari You spend too much time here. These women are just using you.

They don't even show up any more when you're here because they know you'll do all the work.

Sophie And, then, with you. I don't feel like I can trust you. (*Beat.*) You always have these excuses about your phone and your work, but it didn't used to be like that. You used to pick up every time I called and you never used to cancel at the last minute.

Imari Baby, things have been busy for me too.

Sophie I just can't deal with it, on top of everything else. I feel like you're lying to me.

Imari What would I be lying to you about? (*Sophie doesn't respond.*) No, seriously. I think we should talk about this if it's bothering you.

Sophie You've cheated before.

Imari Not with you, not while we were officially in a relationship.

Sophie You always have an excuse.

Imari What are you talking about? We didn't agree that we were monogamous until after the whole thing with Jamie.

Sophie I don't want to hear it. I don't want to talk about it. It's not going to help.

Imari I don't understand you. You want me to talk to you, then you don't.

Sophie Not about this. I don't want to have to talk about this with you. (*Beat.*) I don't want you to cheat.

Imari I haven't. Not while we've been together.

Sophie I don't want to talk about this.

Imari Baby. (*She touches her.*) You're so stressed out. I think you get a little paranoid when you're stressed. (*She kisses her neck.*) Come on. Let's go back to your apartment. (*She kisses her again.*) Don't fight with me about this too.

Sophie I don't want to give you that power over me right now.

Imari Who says it's not you who has the power over me?

Sophie That's a horrible line, Imari.

Imari It's not a line.

Sophie I think it's better if you go.

Imari stands and moves in front of Sophie, takes her hands and pulls her up from the couch, kisses her neck and arms and hands. While this is happening Thea opens the front door and walks in on the two of them, they all see one another and Thea quickly exits.

Projection

Light curtains in front of a window blowing in the breeze.

Sydney (*Recorded.*) I'm not entirely comfortable speaking about intimate love. Writing it down feels too much like confessing. It's too easy to get caught that way. Even with Ruth, I never wrote about it. I suppose I thought that way if anyone ever looked closely at the journals, they would have a hard time figuring out if we were much more than friends. But it seems silly now, looking back—to have denied it. Or to think that people wouldn't immediately understand exactly what kind of relationship we had. (*Beat.*) There was a period where I was afraid of it. Then there was a time when I wished for nothing else, even though I couldn't admit it to Ruth. Then there were times when it was difficult— too difficult. I suppose I don't know whether or not it's different from intimacy with a man. I know a lot of women swear up and down that it is and one is better, but I suppose it's intimacy with another human being either way. I ache for it sometimes. To be able to hold a body in between my arms again—her body. I dream of lying in bed with her at night, her there in front of me, the warmth of her back pressed against my chest, the smell of her neck and her head and her hair. Those are some of the hardest moments. The other kinds of intimacy were good, but my body craves the quiet moments now. That's what I miss most—just lying in bed together. I don't know if that's because I'm a woman. But it's what I feel.

Scene 10

Thea alone.

Thea Sophie? (*Beat.*) Where is she? She should be here by now. (*Beat.*) Popcorn? Popcorn?!

She runs upstairs, bangs on Popcorn's door and yells something. There's a muffled reply. Then we hear Thea stomp back downstairs.

Thea Tell me to go home… (*Beat.*) I can't go home. I don't want to go home. Why should I?

She walks over to the table in the work room and starts pulling things out of the boxes—journals, cassettes. She's throwing them on the floor. Making a mess everywhere. Sophie walks in.

Sophie Thea, what are you doing?

Thea Work, lots of work. I'm working very hard. Just like you. See.

Thea pulls out more journals and throws them on the table, then starts rearranging them and adds more to the disordered pile.

Sophie Thea, stop.

Thea No, you stop. I've got a lot of work to do. I can't talk to you right now. Go sit in a corner by yourself and read something. I don't have time for you. I have important things to do and you're not important.

Sophie What's going on, Thea?

Thea You're late. You said you would be here an hour ago. You never showed up.

Sophie Thea, the Archives isn't even open to the public today.

Thea You said you would be here and that I could stop by and say hello if I wanted to, and I came and you weren't here.

Sophie Why didn't you just go back home?

Thea Because you said you would be here. I needed to see you.

Sophie About what? I'm here now. Why did you need to see me?

Thea No, I'm not going to tell you now, you weren't here. You weren't here when I needed you and now I'm not going to talk to you.

Sophie walks over and tries to start cleaning up the mess Thea has made.

Thea No! Don't touch it. I'm working!

Sophie Thea. You can't treat other people's belongings this way?

Thea This is my place. I spend more time here than anyone. I should get to do whatever I want. I spend more time here than you do. I don't leave to go other places to be with other people. I don't have a girlfriend. I don't have a girlfriend who cheats on me and treats me like a fucking hockey puck.

Beat.

Sophie Thea. Who let you in?

Thea Popcorn.

Sophie What did you tell her?

Thea I told her you told me to meet you here, that I was helping with your project.

Sophie That's not true, Thea. You lied to her.

Thea No, you're the liar. You said you would be here.

Sophie I think you need to calm down and head home, Thea.

Thea Who the fuck are you to tell me to go home?

Sophie Thea, if you don't calm down, I'm going to have to call your mother.

Thea You don't have her number. You're bluffing.

Sophie I do.

Thea How? Where'd you get it?

Sophie Popcorn got it off your cell phone a couple weeks ago.

Thea That's an invasion of privacy. I could call the police.

Sophie You were asleep, it was late, she needed to close up. She was worried about you.

Thea I am going to kill her! (*Beat.*) Popcorn!

Sophie Thea, this isn't a place you can come whenever you want. And it's not really a place to hang out. This is an archive. The things here need to be kept carefully.

Thea You come here whenever you want and do whatever you want.

Sophie You should be spending time with your friends and your family, Thea.

Thea What do you know about it? Are you suddenly my guidance counselor?

Sophie No, Thea, I'm not. That's the problem. I'm not the best person to help you if you're having a hard time.

Thea Ya'll are just a big bunch of white bitches.

Sophie You need to be a little more careful with your words, Thea.

Thea You said this was supposed to be a safe place for people to come to, for people like me. Well, I don't see anyone here like me. I've looked through every one of these damn books and I can't find a single story about anyone like me. And you all pretend like you're all nice and friendly, but when someone really needs something, when someone really needs to be here, they're just shit out of luck.

Sophie Okay, Thea. (*Beat.*) Why did you need me to be here?

Thea No, that's not how this is going to work. You fucked up.

Popcorn comes downstairs.

Popcorn Sorry, ladies. Time to go.

Thea Fuck you.

Popcorn Come again?

Thea You heard me.

Popcorn You need to leave right now.

Thea Make me!

Popcorn I don't play games. You may do that with other people here, but I'll lift you up and throw you out on the street if you talk to me like that. You'll never come in here again.

Sophie She's only fifteen.

Popcorn I don't give a shit. I'm not having it. (*To Thea, getting close to her.*) You need to leave. Right now.

Thea Ugly old bull dyke.

Popcorn (*Moves Thea with her physical presence.*) Go.

Thea I'll come back here and burn this whole fucking place down. (*Popcorn says nothing, just keeps moving her to the door.*) You'll be sorry.

Popcorn gets her out the door and closes and locks it behind her.

Sophie Sorry.

Popcorn You need to stop spending so much time hanging around that little girl.

Sophie I'm sorry. She's so young. She doesn't even know who she is yet.

Popcorn That's not for you to say. Her heart knows, and she's got it bad for you. You hanging around her is making her crazy.

Sophie She's not in love with me.

Popcorn You can fool yourself all you want with that girl you break up with every six days, but you better not fool yourself about that little lady out there. She's madly in love with you, and you spending all that time with her is only making it worse. You're probably her first real love. You've gotta remember how that was. She's got the full crazy. And it's not going to go away any time soon, especially not if you keep letting her think you two are best friends.

Scene 11

Beverly is back at Sydney's door. All we see is the front of the door. She knocks.

Beverly Ms Anders? I was driving by and noticed your light on. I'd like to talk for just a second. (*No response. She knocks again.*) Ms Anders? Can you please come to the door?

We hear Sydney slowly making her way to the door.

Beverly Ms Anders?

We hear Sydney arriving at the door and stopping, she's breathing heavily.

Beverly Ms Anders?

Sydney (*Through the door.*) What is it you want?

Beverly Would you mind just opening the door?

Sydney Who are you?

Beverly My name is Beverly—Beverly Longie. Your friend's daughter, Sarah Epstein, sent me.

Sydney She hasn't been here in months.

Beverly I live close by, she thought I could come and check in on you, since she's been away.

Sydney I don't need checking in on.

Beverly She wanted me to say hello from her, to see if you needed anything. She said she used to go to the grocery store for you, and help you with your laundry.

Sydney I don't need strangers coming into my house.

Beverly I'm a friend, Ms Anders.

Sydney I've never met you.

Beverly Actually, I think we did meet, a couple of years ago, at Izzy's funeral.

Beat.

Sydney I don't remember you.

Beverly How about I stop by this weekend and bring you a couple things. I can drop by the store on my way. Is there anything you need?

Sydney I don't need charity.

Beverly You can pay me. I'll save the receipt.

Sydney I've gotta go.

Beverly How about Sunday afternoon?

Sydney I'm not sure I'll be here.

Beverly Okay. I'll just drop by and see. You sure you don't want me to pick anything up for you? That's when I do my shopping anyhow.

Sydney walks away from the door.

Beverly Good-bye, Ms Anders.

Projection

Looking at pictures of her son, Henry.

Sydney (*Just her voice.*) "They grow up so fast." They always say that. But you don't really realize it until they're grown. When I brought him to college, it nearly broke my heart. I never thought about the fact that he would have to leave. I got so used to him being there. But I couldn't let him know how sad I was to see him go. I wanted him to be happy, to have everything he deserved. That first year was near impossible. I wanted to call him every day, but promised myself that I would wait for him to call. And he did at first, but then the calls started to drop off. And then nothing after the accident. I moved partly because I couldn't get over that feeling that he might call me, even though he was gone. If Ruth hadn't come into my life, I suppose I might have had a hard time keeping on like that, to be alone with that grief. It was frightening sometimes. I'm still not entirely sure how I survived Ruth's death. But you get used it, I suppose. (*Beat.*) That feels like a lie, but I don't really have any idea how else I've managed these years without her.

Scene 12

Sophie and the Volunteer are standing around the table.

Volunteer What is all this?

Sophie A woman sent in her journals and some recordings, and a little bit of poetry. I'm still processing all of it.

Volunteer She anybody famous?

Sophie We haven't looked her up.

Volunteer You haven't Googled her?

Sophie It really doesn't matter. She doesn't need to be famous.

Volunteer goes over to the computer.

Volunteer What's her name?

Sophie I don't think that's necessary.

Volunteer Oh, come on. What's her name?

Sophie Sydney Anders.

Volunteer Is that S-I or S-Y.

Sophie S-Y-D-N-E-Y. Last name A-N-D-E-R-S.

Volunteer Strange name. (*Beat. She types it in and looks through the results.*) Lots of Andersons, Sydney Andrews… I'm not seeing her. (*She types in something more and searches again.*) You said she was a poet?

Sophie She wrote poetry, but I don't know if she was ever published.

Volunteer No, nothing on that either. (*She types more in. Searches again.*) All I get is a white pages result. Does she live in Merrill, Wisconsin? Post Road 342?

Sophie That's where the boxes came from.

Volunteer How did she know to send her stuff in if she's all the way out there in the country? I mean, do you guys send out solicitations or something?

Sophie I imagine she was in touch with someone here a few years ago. Her acquisition form is probably twenty years old. We don't use those ones anymore.

Volunteer Really? Can I see? (*Sophie hands Volunteer one of the acquisition forms.*) How old do you think she is? Or do you think she passed away and her family sent this stuff in for her?

Sophie I don't know.

Volunteer Don't you have to find that out at some point?

Sophie I'll do some research when I'm done writing all this stuff up. I've just been busy with other things.

Volunteer Sorry, I'm being pushy. I get excited. What can I help you with?

Sophie What were you working on last time you were here?

Volunteer The subject files.

Sophie There's always more to do in the subject files. The stack is in that cubby over there.

Volunteer You don't need help with these journals?

Sophie Not right now, thanks.

Volunteer Okay.

The Volunteer walks over, takes up the pile of papers that Sophie pointed to and walks into the main room of the library to start sorting through them.

Scene 13

Thea is at the front door. Imari is outside.

Thea She's not here.

Imari Just let me in.

Thea I said, she's not here and the Archives is closed.

Imari Then what are you doing here?

Thea Volunteering. It's a special workday.

Imari Well, then I'm here to help.

Thea No, you're not. You've never helped out around here. You just come in here to distract Sophie and try to convince her to take you back.

Imari Excuse me?

Imari enters.

Thea You're not supposed to be in here.

Imari Well then, neither are you.

Thea I could go up and get Popcorn and have her kick you out.

Imari You wouldn't do that. You're afraid of her. And she's just as likely to kick you out as me.

Thea Why are you such a jerk?

Imari Excuse me?

Thea You're a jerk to me, you're a jerk to Sophie. And I saw you in the coffee shop a few weeks ago and you were a jerk to the guy behind the counter there too.

Imari And you think you're not a jerk?

Thea Fuck you!

Imari I don't even understand what a kid like you gets out of a place like this? All these dusty books about boring old women who most people don't even know. You live in New York City. Why would you choose to come here all the time? You should be out with your friends. That's what teenagers are supposed to do.

Thea You don't know anything about my life. And you obviously don't know much if you think these books are just old and dusty and have nothing to do with you.

Imari Yeah, right, these women fought for me. Great. Thank you very much. That doesn't mean I want to sit around and read their bad poetry and learn about their sad lives.

Thea You're an idiot.

Imari How about I go up there myself and get Popcorn? How about that?

Popcorn enters.

Popcorn No need. I'm right here. And I think both of you should leave. The workday was canceled. You'll need to go. (*To Thea.*) And I'm not even going to ask you how you got in here. Which is why you are going to leave right now, without saying any thing to me about it. (*Beat.*) Both of you. Go. This is not some lesbian bar where you can air out your shit for everyone else to see. (*Thea and Imari head towards the door.*) Crazy fools, a grown woman and a teenager fighting over a woman who could do better than both of you. Please do not come back. (*She closes the door behind them. The phone rings. Popcorn makes her way over to answer it.*) Yes, Sophie, I just kicked both of your girlfriends out. You need to deal with them and you need to keep your shit out of the Archives, okay? You need to tell them to stop meeting you here because I'm sick of having to handle this for you. (*Beat.*) Yes, you should. (*Beat.*) That's not my problem. (*Beat.*) Sophie, look, you're a very nice girl, but I think you can be a little naïve about people and I'm sorry your friends and family aren't telling you this but Imari is taking advantage of you all the time. (*Beat.*) Yes, I did have a shitty night, but that doesn't change the situation. What I'm telling you is the truth. And somebody needs to have told it to you a while ago. (*Beat.*) I'm sorry, Sophie. I don't want to be involved in your personal life, but you bring it in here with you every time you come and so everyone else here has to deal with it. I don't think you see that.

Scene 14

Beverly at Sydney's door. She has a bag of groceries in her arms. She knocks.

Beverly Ms Anders. It's Beverly. I stopped at the grocery store, got you a couple things I thought you might like. (*No response. She knocks again.*) Ms Anders. It's Beverly, from Monday afternoon.

Sydney slowly makes her way to the door.

Beverly Ms Anders? May I give you these groceries?

Sydney unlatches the door and opens it.

Beverly Hello. It's very nice to meet you. (*Sydney doesn't respond.*) I've got a few things here. Sarah said you were a tea drinker, so I brought you a couple of my favorites. And some shortbread and chocolates to go with it. Then some fruit and eggs, because who doesn't need eggs?

Sydney reaches out for the bag.

Beverly Oh, it's a little heavy. I can carry it in. I thought maybe I could use your bathroom, if that's okay? I've been running errands all morning.

Sydney pauses for a moment, then lets Beverly in. The Archives becomes the inside of Sydney's home. Beverly sets the bag of groceries down on the table with Sydney's journals.

Sydney The bathroom is just down the hall.

Beverly Thank you. I'll just be one minute.

Beverly leaves to use the rest room. Sydney starts to unpack the bag, folding it up once she's placed all the items on the counter. Beverly then returns from the bathroom.

Beverly Thank you so much. It's frustrating that none of those stores have public restrooms.

Sydney Thank you for these things.

Beverly It's no problem.

Sydney How much money do you need?

Beverly Oh, please, nothing. If you want to share a cup of tea though, I wouldn't say no to that.

Sydney I don't have anywhere comfortable for you to sit.

Beverly walks over to the small table with a single chair.

Beverly Is there another chair in the house, or a little box? I don't mind sitting on whatever. I'm not fancy.

Sydney pauses for a moment.

Sydney I could bring something in.

Beverly Just point me in the right direction, I can go get it.

Sydney You put the water on. Here's the kettle. (*She points to the kettle on the stovetop.*)

Beverly Great.

Sydney exits. Beverly picks up the teakettle, brings it to the sink and fills it up. Then sets it onto the stove to boil. With that done she looks around the room. She sees some photographs on the table and stands as she looks down at them.

Sydney Here you go.

Sydney has retrieved a chair and sets it at the small table.

Beverly These are great photographs. Are they your family?

Sydney Everyone in my family is dead except me.

Beverly I'm sorry to hear that. (*Beat.*) Thank you for the chair.

Sydney What kind of tea do you want?

Beverly I brought a ginger mint that I love. If you wanted to have that, I could make us two cups.

Sydney I'll do it.

Beverly Thank you so much.

Beat.

Beverly I know I mentioned my name last time I was at the door, but maybe I ought to properly introduce myself. I'm Beverly Longie.

Sydney doesn't offer a hand or any greeting in particular, just continues going about making tea—getting cups from the cabinet, opening the box of tea and pulling out two bags.

Sydney Sydney.

Beverly Very nice to meet you. (*Beat.*) Sarah had such nice things to say about you.

Sydney I haven't seen her in over a year.

Beverly She's at school now. She got into the University of Michigan with a scholarship. I think she's studying to be a veterinarian, or maybe a physical therapist, or both. I can't remember.

Sydney She used to come by here, after her mother passed.

Beverly Yes, she said she remembers you through her whole childhood, always stopping by here with her mother. She talked about the dinners you and Ruth used to host. She remembered staying up for hours while all of you talked. She said she would always fall asleep to the sound of your voices, with her head on her mother's lap.

Sydney Ruth passed away eight years ago.

Beverly Yes, she mentioned that. I'm sorry, I shouldn't have brought it up. It was just such a nice memory.

Sydney How did you come to know Sarah?

Beverly After her mother passed away. She was only seventeen at the time. I was the caseworker assigned to her.

Sydney You're a social worker?

Beverly Yes.

Sydney Is that why you're here?

Beverly No. I came because Sarah told me about you and wondered if we might get along. I meant to come earlier, but with my work schedule…

Sydney Did she think I might be dead out here?

The teakettle whistles and Sydney pours water into the cups, bringing one to Beverly.

Beverly Nothing like that. She just mentioned that we had a few things in common and that we lived near to one another.

Sydney Mmm.

Sydney brings the other cup over and sits down at the table with Beverly.

Beverly Thanks so much. It's starting to get blustery out there and a hot cup of tea does such a good job of keeping off the chill. (*Beat.*) How long have you been in this house?

Sydney I don't know. Thirty years.

Beverly I've only been here eight years. I came over from North Dakota.

Sydney That where you're from?

Beverly Yeah, Spirit Lake.

Sydney You're Indian?

Beverly Dakota.

Sydney Why'd you move out here?

Beverly My partner.

Sydney Your husband, you mean?

Beverly No, my wife.

Sydney Is that why Sarah thought we would get along?

Beverly That wasn't the only reason.

Sydney No?

Beverly Poetry, tea, birds.

Sydney You're a birdwatcher?

Beverly Not so much a watcher. I just like them. Always have. As a little kid I memorized every bird and every bit of information in one of the guidebooks we had in our school library. I've loved them ever since I saw my first one.

Sydney I have brown thrashers along the drive. They've been nesting there for as long as I've lived here.

Beverly Sarah mentioned it. I'd love to see them.

Sydney You can walk there.

Beverly Would you like to walk down there with me?

Sydney I've already taken my walk this morning.

Beverly I'd be happy to walk out with you some other time, or go for a drive. The ridge along fifty-five is just gorgeous right now.

Sydney No, thank you.

Beverly nods. Looks at the photos on the table.

Beverly Is that Sarah?

Sydney Where?

Beverly In this one.

Beverly hands Sydney one of the photos.

Sydney Yes. That's her, with her mother.

Beverly I thought so. She must only be seven or eight in that picture. (*Beat.*) Who are those other women?

Sydney A couple of other friends. Ruth used to get everyone together. I never would have had that many people over. She loved the company. I preferred it to be just us.

Beverly As I understand it, she had friends all over the area who came to those dinners.

Sydney From as far as Des Moines, every Sunday night. But that stopped when Ruth passed.

Beat.

Beverly Do you think you'll stay up here?

Sydney Where else would I go?

Projection

Stirring tea in a cup with a spoon. Sydney now sits alone at the table.

Sydney (*Recorded.*) She said she was the welcome committee. She heard I was from Pittsburgh and wanted to make sure I had a few important things. She brought me emergency candles, some seeds for a garden, a loaf of bread, and an axe—a brand new one. She even offered to show me how to use it. She asked me how I'd heard about Merrill, Wisconsin. I made something up. I couldn't tell her the truth—one of the other women at the YWCA had been there to visit her boyfriend's family and said she'd never been anywhere so isolated in all her life. (*Beat.*) She shook my hand that first time we met. I can still remember the feeling of her palm on mine. I wouldn't let myself believe that she was like me, but I think she suspected me right away. I'm sure she saw it in my eyes. She dropped in on me every week for a couple of months after that before inviting me to join one of her dinners. I'd never met another lesbian, not a real one, not one that I could sit and talk to, that I could look at, who actually called herself a lesbian. She was beautiful. (*Beat.*) I remember thinking, how could she suddenly appear? As if that kind of love had been a possibility all along.

Scene 15

Sophie sits at the large table reading one of Sydney's journals. Popcorn walks in on her way to the kitchen. She stops.

Popcorn Working late?

Sophie Sorry. I can go.

Popcorn Oh please. I don't care. You're not the one that's the trouble—it's those other two who are always chasing after you.

Sophie I'm really sorry about all that.

Popcorn What are you gonna do? Lesbians are crazy. (*Sophie responds silently, then goes back to the journal.*) What is all that mess anyway?

Sophie Journals and recordings that someone sent in.

Popcorn Anyone I would know?

Sophie No, I doubt it.

Popcorn Is she still alive?

Sophie I haven't figured that out yet. There's not much indication. The journals go up to 2010, but then these tapes are dated up until just before the packages were sent, so I'm assuming that she's still alive, or that if she passed, it only just happened.

Popcorn There wasn't a note anywhere in the packages?

Sophie Just an old acquisition form. (*She hands the form to Popcorn.*)

Popcorn That's odd. She must have been thinking about submitting this stuff for a long time. I wonder who sent her the forms. Cassidy or Helen might have known her.

Sophie I should ask them next time they're here. It would be interesting to know what led her to contribute her stuff. I mean, they say everyone is welcome to do it, but so few people actually do. I would think it's a pretty difficult thing—to expose yourself like that. To let people make judgments about you, to let them decide what kind of person you were.

Popcorn Yeah, I think a lot of Cassidy and Helen's friends sent things in right after they bought this building, but since then it's mainly been famous people or writers, and even then, it's not that many, because the really famous ones send their stuff to universities.

Sophie It's interesting—this woman's story. I'm still piecing it together, but from what I understand, her brother died when she was a teenager—he was older and I'm pretty sure he was gay, though she never uses that word. She thinks he killed himself, but she doesn't know for sure—he drowned, when he was seventeen. Then, right before her 18th birthday she ran away to Pittsburgh. Something seems to have happened back home, but I haven't figured out what—she doesn't talk about it in the journals, all her writing is really guarded. Maybe the tapes are different. She gave herself a new name in Pittsburgh—Sydney Anders, but she doesn't say what her old name was. Then somehow her sister ended up finding her. She'd gotten pregnant—the sister—and didn't want her family to figure it out, so she convinced Sydney to take the baby. I'm about eight years in now—she's had the baby for about six years. She named him Henry.

Popcorn Is she out?

Sophie She never mentions love at all, except how much she loves the baby. For awhile she was living at a YWCA and she talks a lot about the other women there, but it's mostly gossip. I don't think she saw herself as a lesbian at the time. She knew she was different, but I'm not sure she had any real contact with other lesbians, or with the whole idea. I think she just thought that she wasn't interested in love the way the other women were—not love with a man.

Popcorn What year?

Sophie This entry is August 8, 1951.

Popcorn Are you going to read every single one?

Sophie No, I don't suppose so. I mean, I skim some of them, but it's interesting, you know. It's not a story I've heard before.

Popcorn (*Looking through the cassettes.*) We should listen to one of these tapes.

Sophie I didn't want to have to drag that old stereo out of the basement.

Popcorn There's a tape recorder in here. (*She walks over to the desk, opens one of the drawers and pulls out an old portable tape recorder.*) Frances likes to use it when she's putting together her lists.

Sophie That's so funny.

Popcorn Whatever works.

Popcorn walks over and chooses a tape from the pile, opens it and inserts it into the tape recorder and presses play.

Sydney (*Recorded. Projection of water fades in as the monologue continues.*) Ruth wanted half of her ashes spread in the river back in Wyoming, and the other half here on our land. It took me two days to drive over there. It could have taken less, but I wasn't used to the roads and wasn't used to driving alone for any distance. I told them at the entrance what I came for. I had called ahead and spoken to a woman there who had gone to school with her. She said she would meet me when I came. I tried to say no, but I didn't have the words. I didn't even know if they knew about Ruth. She said she had been open about herself back there, that they all knew, but still, I wasn't certain. When I got there, the man at the gates said that I should drive up to the river and there would be a couple of people there to meet me. I wished I could have turned around. I wished I had never come. But Ruth wanted so much for part of her to go back there, she'd spoken to me about it many times. There were two trucks parked by the water and three people standing not far from the shore, waiting for me. I had never seen them before, though I thought I recognized one of them from Ruth's photographs. We didn't speak much, just said hello and walked to the edge of the water. I had never done that before—spread someone's ashes. When Henry died I had him buried near the school—close to his friends. They wanted to be near to him, and I wanted him to be near to them, not out here. (*Beat.*) I suppose it was clear to the people from the reservation that I didn't know what to do. The woman—she took the urn from me. I was thankful, it felt like something too heavy to hold. I was afraid to open it, to think about what was inside. (*Beat.*) She spread some in the wind and out on the water, and then each of the men followed, doing the same. When they were done, they handed the urn back to me. I did the same. I don't know if they prayed to themselves while they did it or not. I don't know what was in my head. I feel like there was a blankness, that there was nothing there. They invited me to join them for food and drinks after, but I couldn't. There was a bench nearby and I sat for hours, just watching the water. It was dark when I finally left. I drove all the way home that night, got in by morning the next day. (*Beat.*) She was gone. I suppose whatever higher power there was could only let me love one thing at a time. First my brother Gio. Then Henry. Then Ruth. I knew that with her I had all the love that I had been allotted in my life. And even that seemed like more than I deserved. So, I stayed up here on my own. I had already been so separate. I didn't want to have to explain myself anymore, or leave blanks in my sentences, tell lies. Ruth hated that I would do it, but I couldn't face them, I couldn't bear the way they would look at me, the way everything changed when they knew that about me. I was more comfortable when people thought I was just Henry's mother—a lonely, single woman with a child. That was easier for me. Now I can be just as I like out here. No one sees me. No one needs to figure out what I am to them, what I mean, what slot I fit in.

Scene 16

Beverly and Sydney are sitting in Sydney's kitchen—the Archives' kitchen.

Sydney You've never said much about your wife.

Beverly Gail? She passed about two years ago…two years ago next month—the twenty-third.

Sydney I'm sorry.

Beverly We had many good years together.

Sydney It was just the two of you?

Beverly She had children from her first marriage, to a man. They were married fifteen years, right after high school.

Sydney When did you—

Beverly Oh, I didn't meet her until well after all that. It was someone else that she left the marriage for, but the other woman wouldn't leave her husband. It was a mess from what I understand. Each of them had children and families. But in the end, the other woman just couldn't do it, she didn't have the will to leave her life behind. She wouldn't risk it. So Gail was left on her own.

Sydney Where did you meet her?

Beverly A support group run by the Alliance. We had to meet in people's homes back then because no one was willing to host us. We advertised in the back of *The Ladder* and a couple of other local women's newsletters. It was supposed to be a political group, but more than anything we just wanted to be around other people like us, that we thought were like us anyway.

Sydney What about on the reservation?

Beverly You know, it's a very old culture out there. Trying to hold onto something that precarious isn't easy. It's made a lot of them very conservative. They didn't try to deny it out of existence, but they weren't really all that keen to accept us either.

Sydney You were together for awhile?

Beverly Twenty-four years. We lived together for twenty, give or take. I traveled a lot for work—I used to coordinate a couple of programs at reservations across the North.

Sydney Ever work in northern Montana?

Beverly Oh sure. Fort Peck. Fort Belknap. A lot of trips to the Blackfoot Reservation.

Sydney Ruth was born there.

Beverly At Blackfoot?

Sydney nods.

Beverly It's beautiful up there. Did she stay for long?

Sydney When she was twelve her mother and father left to try to find work. They traveled all over. They would only go back for visits. I think she always wanted to go back. I think it's why once she became a professor she decided to moved as close as she could get. She would go there and help out on her breaks. They knew her pretty well.

Beat. Sydney drinks her tea.

Beverly I had to move out of our house. It was just too big for me on my own and too much work. And with the kids so far away now, there wasn't much point in keeping their rooms.

Sydney I'm not moving.

Beverly Oh, I won't try to convince you of that.

Sydney No?

Beverly As long as you don't mind me coming out here to visit, I'm not going to try to convince you of anything.

Sydney Why do you come out here?

Beverly Well, I was thinking we might have started to become friends.

Sydney Hmm.

Beverly Does it bother you when I come out here?

Sydney Not particularly.

Beverly Well, good then. I like it. It's a nice break from all the straight biddies in town who make such a fuss over me being single and still working.

Sydney Hmm.

Beverly Well, I better get going. (*She stands up, goes to her bag and pulls out a card, which she hands to Sydney.*) Here's my number. Just call me if you need anything, or want me to pick anything up before I come out here next time.

Sydney Thank you.

Beverly See you next weekend?

Sydney Okay.

Beverly Want me to bring anything special?

Sydney You don't have any cardboard boxes, do you?

Beverly Like moving boxes?

Sydney For mailing—maybe the size of a small moving box. I had some in the basement, but they were all damp. I had to throw them in the burn pile.

Beverly I'm sure I've got something, or I can always run by the post office.

Sydney Don't go to any trouble.

Beverly I'm there every other day anyway, it's no trouble.

Sydney Thanks.

Beverly How many?

Sydney Five or six, I guess.

Beverly Okay. See you next week.

Sydney stands.

Sydney Yes.

Beverly Bye.

Beverly walks out the front door and Sydney closes the door behind her, then walks back into the kitchen to wash up. When she's done she turns off all the lights and exits.

Scene 17

Thea is at the Archives' front door picking the lock. The place is dark. She eventually gets in. She walks around leaving the lights off, picking a few things up, eating a cookie left out from the last scene. Then she walks into the main reading room. She runs her fingers along the shelves and then stops. She tries to reach up to a book on a high shelf, but she can't reach it. She turns to get a chair, which she places beside the shelf so she can climb up. As she's reaching Sophie comes to the front door and unlocks it. Hearing the door, Thea jumps down and runs back into the kitchen to hide. Sophie enters, turning on the lights. As she walks in she notices the chair out of place and puts it back where it ought to be. Then she walks in to the main work room. She sets her bag down and takes off her jacket. After doing this, she walks into the kitchen, where she's startled by Thea, who has just jammed herself against a wall.

Sophie Oh my god, Thea! What are you doing here? You scared me.

Thea I just dropped by to pick something up.

Sophie goes to the sink to wash her hands and put hot water on for tea.

Sophie How did you get in here?

Thea Popcorn let me in.

Sophie She couldn't have. I just spoke to her on the phone. She's at the airport right now.

Thea She let me in before she left.

Sophie stops what she's doing.

Sophie Thea, did you break in here?

Thea No! What the hell? You think I'm some kind of thief? Don't tell me after all this that you're a racist.

Sophie Why were you hiding in the dark when I came in here?

Thea The lights weren't working.

Sophie Thea, I trusted you. I even stood up for you.

Thea Oh please. Don't act like you were doing me any favors.

Sophie You should probably leave.

Thea Yeah, fine.

Thea walks into the main reading room, puts the chair back where she had it before and climbs back onto it. Sophie is watching. Thea reaches up toward the shelf.

Sophie You can't steal these books, Thea. They're donations.

Thea I'm not stealing your damn books.

Thea pulls a handful of books off the shelf with one hand and then reaches into the space left on the shelf with the other, retrieving a composition book. She puts the books back where they were, gets down from the chair, and she begins to walk to the front door.

Sophie What is that?

Thea Nothing.

Sophie Does it belong to you?

Thea I'm not aware of any other Thea Goldfarb that comes in here.

Sophie Is that your diary?

Thea I'm not eight years old. I don't keep a diary.

Sophie What is it?

Thea I thought you wanted me to leave? I'm a criminal, remember.

Sophie Thea, I need to know what it is you're taking.

Thea It's my journal, okay! I left it here. I had to come back and get it. I didn't think anybody would be here. It's not supposed to be open. I waited until Popcorn left and then I jimmied the lock, okay. But only to get this and leave and never come back. Does that answer all your questions?

Sophie You did break in.

Thea I had to get my stuff. I will never, ever come back to this fucking place, okay.

Sophie What is going on with you, Thea? What are you doing breaking into buildings?

Thea It's not like a habit, okay. I learned to do it at my house 'cause I always forget my keys. And it's not like I'm stealing anything. I just came to get my own stuff and leave.

Sophie But if somebody saw you doing that, they might call the cops.

Thea Why, 'cause I'm black?

Sophie Because you're breaking and entering.

Thea You're such a jerk.

Sophie doesn't reply to this.

Thea I thought before that it was Imari and Popcorn who were the jerks, but now I see it's really you.

Sophie stays quiet.

Thea Come on, say something. I know you want to.

Beat.

Sophie I'm not really sure what to say.

Thea 'Cause I'm so dumb? 'Cause I'm such a problem for everyone? 'Cause you hate me so much you don't even want to talk to me any more?

Sophie No, Thea. I just want you to take a minute and calm down.

Thea I'm fifteen. I can't calm down. That's for you grown-ups. I don't know how to calm down. Everything feels crazy all the time to me, because it is.

Beat.

Sophie I felt like that when I was your age.

Thea Don't ever say that, you can't ever know how I feel.

Sophie Everybody goes through their own struggles, Thea. That's all I meant.

Thea My struggles will never be like yours. Never.

Sophie Damn it, I'm sorry, I just…

Thea I need to go home. My parents are expecting me.

Sophie Okay.

Beat.

Thea Why are you even here anyway?

Sophie I've got to write a paper for school and I told Popcorn I'd take care of the schedule for next month, and Cassidy needed me to send her the notes from our last meeting.

Thea Why do you do that? Why do you do other people's work for them when you already have too much to do?

Sophie sits down.

Sophie Because I'm avoiding the things I don't want to deal with.

Thea Finally. The truth.

Sophie I shouldn't be talking with you about this.

Thea Why? Because you think I can't understand? I'm too young? Too stupid?

Sophie No, Thea. Because of what happened earlier.

Thea What are you talking about?

Sophie When you lost your temper. When Popcorn had to ask you to leave.

Thea What about it? I got angry. So what?

Sophie Why were you so angry?

Thea I was just pissed off, okay.

Sophie But why were you pissed off?

Thea What are you trying to say?

Sophie It seems like it might have had something to do with me.

Thea What—like I'm in love with you? I can't believe you. I can't believe you would say that!

Sophie I didn't say that, Thea. You did.

Long beat.

Sophie Thea, I really like our friendship, and I think you probably know that it can never be more than that.

Thea I hate all you people. I can't believe I've wasted so much time here.

Sophie Thea.

Thea Fuck you.

Thea leaves, slamming the door behind her.

Projection

Sydney's hands in the sink—she's washing ink from her skin. We see this for a few beats before the voice over begins.

Sydney Would I have done it differently if I could? I wouldn't have known how. And it makes it seem like I've been unhappy all this time, which isn't true. (*Beat.*) Mostly I just wish Gio could have been here. He would have been braver than me, I think. Somehow I imagine him with people all around him all the time, like Ruth. That's just how some people are. Henry was a little bit like that. I would just sit and marvel at it sometimes, all those friends and girls fawning all over him. Once in awhile I would imagine myself as a great lover, with girls chasing after me—a great Lothario. Who doesn't want to be someone else now and again? To try out a different life; a different costume.

Scene 18

Popcorn unlocks the front door. Imari is behind her.

Popcorn I doubt she's here. I haven't heard from her since I left.

Imari I can't find her and she won't answer her phone.

Popcorn Did you two break up?

Imari Did she say that to you?

Popcorn Didn't I just say I haven't spoken to her since I left?

Imari Well, if you haven't spoken to her, then how do you know that she's not here?

Popcorn See for yourself.

Imari walks around the main floor, then runs upstairs. She doesn't find Sophie anywhere. Popcorn picks the mail up off the floor and brings it, along with her rolling suitcase, into the work room. She's going through the mail when Imari comes back downstairs.

Imari She's not here.

Popcorn Well, have a nice evening.

Imari Where is she?

Popcorn How would I know? I'm not her keeper.

Imari You act like you know everything. I would assume you would also know where she is.

Popcorn Aren't you her girlfriend?

Imari You just said she and I broke up.

Popcorn (*Still sorting through the mail.*) You can let yourself out.

Imari When is she coming back?

Popcorn (*Pointing, but not looking up.*) The door is just through there.

Imari You can think whatever you want about me, but she chose to be in a relationship with me. I'm not some monster who came and seduced her and made her be with me.

Popcorn doesn't respond.

Imari Yeah, well, where's your fucking girlfriend?

Popcorn As of this morning, Indonesia.

Imari Fucking some other chick, no doubt. Glad to see your sorry ass leave.

Popcorn (*Finally looks up, but calmly.*) Do you think that by saying that you're going to make me dislike you more than I already do? Is that your intention?

Imari You are such a stuck-up, aloof asshole.

Popcorn Good-bye, Imari.

Imari No, you wanna get into it, let's get into it.

Popcorn I do not want to get into it, Imari. I just got off a 15-hour flight. I'd prefer not to deal with anyone right now. There wasn't supposed to be anyone here when I came home. The person you really want to fight with isn't here. And I'm not going to act as a stand-in for you.

Sophie comes to the door, unlocks it and enters.

Sophie Imari, what are you doing here?

Popcorn I'm going to leave you two alone.

Sophie (*To Popcorn.*) But I need to talk to you about the computer upstairs.

Popcorn Come find me when you two are done with whatever this is. I can't promise I'll be awake.

Popcorn stands, takes her bag and goes upstairs.

Sophie Imari…

Imari I've been trying to get in touch with you for days. I looked everywhere for you.

Sophie Why?

Imari Because I love you and I don't want to break up.

Sophie But I do.

Imari No, you don't. You're just stressed out and you were angry and you have every right to be. But you don't really want to break up with me. I love you. You love me.

Sophie No. I don't love you. I already told you that. Not anymore.

Imari Don't say that. You're breaking my heart. (*Beat.*) Why do you want to hurt me like this?

Sophie That's not going to work anymore.

Imari Well, what will? Tell me and I'll do it.

Sophie Nothing.

Imari I don't believe you. This isn't you. You're not acting like you.

Sophie walks to the mail pile that Popcorn left on the table.

Imari You'll never see me again.

Sophie says nothing.

Imari What about all your stuff?

Sophie I took it with me when I left the other night.

Imari What about my stuff?

Sophie I already put it in a box and left it at Greta's.

Imari Just like that? You just cut if off? Like you've been planning it for weeks?

Sophie I can't even count the number of times we've broken up before.

Imari But you always come back.

Beat.

Imari What am I supposed to do now?

Beat.

Imari I love you.

Beat.

Imari You're not going to say anything?

Sophie I don't think there's anything I can say, Imari.

Imari You want me to just go?

Sophie This is my place to come to, okay. This is where I get away. I need for this to remain my place.

Imari So, like I should never come here?

Sophie You never did before.

Imari But, I'm going to miss you. I already do.

Sophie nods.

Imari Fine. That's how you want this to go.

Imari pauses for awhile before she leaves. Sophie sits down at the table after the front door closes. After a few long beats Popcorn comes downstairs.

Popcorn I saw her walking down the front stairs.

Beat.

Popcorn You okay?

Sophie tries to speak, but can't. Popcorn walks over next to her.

Popcorn You did the right thing.

Sophie I hate her so much. Why did she make me fall in love with her?

Popcorn We don't have to talk about it. It's okay to just let it be.

Sophie I don't want to cry about it anymore. I've been crying over her for almost a year now. I want to get angry and throw things and scream at her.

Popcorn You're going to have to go somewhere else if you want to do that.

Sophie sits down.

Sophie I don't want to be a mess anymore. That whole relationship was a mess.

Popcorn You've already come a long way if you can see that.

Sophie Apparently women who look at me can just see it written all over me. Insecure, shy, bookish lesbian—free to be taken advantage of, willing to be walked all over, too eager to please, repressed.

Popcorn Is that all?

Sophie I'm serious.

Popcorn You're not that way with me. You're not that way with anybody else here. You're only that way when you meet a woman who also happens to be an asshole.

Sophie I'm such a type.

Popcorn You need to be a little less hard on yourself.

Sophie How are you not hard on yourself? How do you manage this stuff?

Popcorn I used to be plenty hard on myself. But I decided I wasn't going to do it anymore. I wasn't going to feel the way everyone thought I ought to feel or be, because I was black, because I'm a dyke. I decided I'd rather enjoy my life as much as possible and forget all of them.

Sophie Just like that?

Popcorn Sure, I just waved this little magic wand and all the pain went away and never came back again. Just like in the fairy tales.

Sophie Well, then, you should wave it over me.

Popcorn It's not easy for any of us, Sophie. But when you can stop doing things that are making you unhappy, you should—it's a privilege not everyone has.

Beat.

Sophie Thea broke in here the other day.

Popcorn Did you call the police?

Sophie She just wanted a journal she'd left here.

Popcorn Is that all she took?

Sophie Yeah. I was here.

Popcorn Are you sure?

Sophie She wasn't trying to steal anything.

Popcorn You don't think that little girl is playing you a little?

Sophie Not right now, Popcorn.

Popcorn I'm sorry. It's just that girl is trying really hard to get herself into some serious trouble. She needs to understand there are consequences for some of the shit she pulls.

Sophie I tried to talk to her.

Popcorn You can't talk to a fifteen year old who is in love with you.

Sophie You said I needed to talk to her.

Popcorn Not after she breaks in to this place just so she can be close to you.

Sophie It was her journal she came for.

Popcorn You lesbians never learn.

Sophie You're a lesbian too.

Popcorn I live in the Lesbian Archives, for God's sake—I know I'm a lesbian. Most of the time I feel like I can't get away from lesbians. She's fifteen. She's probably just had her heart broken for the first time by a woman. She's not going to want to be your friend after that. She might not ever want to see you again. That's not something most people want to revisit over and over again.

Sophie I just don't want her to lose this place. It seems like she really needs somewhere to go and it's better she come here than a lot of other places.

Popcorn She's a kid living in New York City, she's going to get into trouble no matter what.

Sophie She doesn't fit in at school, her parents aren't there for her right now.

Popcorn Sophie. I've never met a black butch lesbian that fit in much of anywhere. She's gonna have to start figuring that out sooner or later. People out there are gonna have a million and sixty different names for her, almost all of which are gonna be painful. Hiding from that isn't gonna make it easier to deal with. None of us fit in, especially not at that age. You eventually learn that's not the point.

Sophie At least she feels safe here.

Popcorn I give up.

Popcorn stands up, but looks over at the boxes of Sydney's stuff.

Popcorn Haven't you been working on these journals for a while now?

Sophie I keep getting caught up reading them.

Popcorn I would never send my stuff in to this place.

Sophie But you live here?

Popcorn The rent is cheap.

Sophie Oh, come on, it's more than that.

Popcorn I have slept with a handful of the women who come in here.

Sophie Not all of us can match your charms.

Popcorn It just comes natural.

Sophie How's Rachel?

Popcorn She's good. I think it's been really good for her to be out there.

Sophie How is it for you?

Popcorn Some days good, some days not so good.

Sophie When does she come back?

Popcorn April.

Sophie That's a long way off.

Popcorn It's not as far away as it was when she left.

Sophie Do you worry about her?

Popcorn Of course, I love her. (*Beat.*) Sometimes I think she's safer out there than we are here.

Beat.

Popcorn You know, relationships aren't easy for anyone I know, Sophie. Not anyone.

Sophie I guess I want to believe someone has figured it out.

Popcorn As far as I can tell, that's just now how it works.

Sophie This woman, the one who wrote the journals, she lost her brother, then her son, then her partner. She lives alone now, somewhere in northern Wisconsin, if she's still alive.

Popcorn I could never live alone. Even if I'd been hurt like that.

Sophie You think?

Popcorn I'd be afraid by myself.

Sophie She lived there with her partner before, in the same house.

Popcorn The isolation would get to me.

Sophie I think she prefers it because she doesn't have to deal with anyone else—she doesn't have to worry about what they think of her or about becoming attached and then losing someone else again.

Popcorn Who doesn't? She probably didn't even fully understand who she was.

Sophie Yeah. It took me awhile.

Popcorn And even then you're always finding out new things—nothing is fixed, nothing is stable. At least that's my experience.

Sophie I can't help wondering about her—what people must have thought of her—you know. What did her family think? Did they just think she was a reject—a bad egg? Or was it more complicated than that? Like they knew they couldn't handle it themselves, so they pushed her away. And then her son? He died at twenty. Did he ever think of her as anything other than his mother? He never knew her as anything else. She never dated while he was alive, she never spoke to him about love. At least it doesn't seem like it, not from her own experience. I can't imagine she would have ever used the word lesbian with him—she barely uses it in her journal. (*Beat.*) It makes me wonder what else she still might be leaving out? I don't have a picture of her face in my mind. It's like with Imari and I, we talked all the time, I know how she talked to me, and I know how she talked about herself, but I'm not sure I could describe her in words that would fit. I'm not sure I would know which categories to put her in.

Popcorn Cheater, for one.

Sophie Okay.

Popcorn Sorry—you laid that one out for me.

Beat.

Popcorn I'm exhausted. I should get to bed.

Popcorn begins to exit to upstairs.

Sophie Hey, wait, how was your trip?

Popcorn Good. It was awkward at first. She's changed, even in three months. I think maybe I've changed a little bit too. It's strange to see someone you know that well becoming something different.

Sophie How has she changed? It hasn't been that long.

Popcorn She's more confident, calmer. She's also thinner—the food out there hasn't been good for her. She's still Rachel—but she's different. She's aged a little bit too. She was nervous being at the hotel—I think it's probably just a shock to go from the camps to civilization. It took a little while to really recognize each other, to be comfortable, to get back into a rhythm. (*Beat.*) That's just it, right? Even something you feel certain you've figured out, that you've paid a lot of attention to, and cared for, and looked after, even that changes.

Sophie You seem so calm and philosophical about it.

Popcorn I'm just tired.

Sophie But even before the trip.

Popcorn Oh, that's lots of therapy, alcohol, Buddhism, good food, hot baths, and friends who keep me from losing my mind.

Sophie I didn't know you were a Buddhist.

Popcorn There aren't many of us, but black Buddhists do exist.

Sophie Well, welcome home.

Popcorn Call me if you need to.

Sophie Thanks.

Popcorn But give me like 24 hours to catch up on my sleep, okay?

Sophie Good night.

Popcorn Night.

Popcorn goes back upstairs.

Scene 19

Beverly is taping up one of the boxes. Sydney is packing another.

Beverly How did you even find out about this place?

Sydney Ruth. She gave them as much money as she could when they were trying to buy a building. I think she met one of the ladies who founded it. She sent some of her things, but she didn't keep journals or anything like that—she was always too busy talking with people, being out in the world. She made me promise I would send my stuff. She even called and got the forms for me and everything. She made me swear.

Beverly Why now? I mean, wouldn't you rather wait?

Sydney I don't want someone else doing this after I die. I don't want them to send the wrong things or to forget it or leave it unfinished. Besides, I can barely stand to write anymore—my hands and my eyes are getting worse. I've just been recording the tapes.

Beverly Are you doing okay, Sydney? I worry about you sometimes.

Sydney I've been taking care of myself just fine these past 87 years. I think I'll manage just fine a few more.

Beverly Do you get to the doctor at all?

Sydney I don't need a caretaker, Beverly. I told you when we first met, if that's why you're here, you should leave now.

Beverly I know, Syd. (*Beat.*) I just want you to know you don't have to be alone out here. My guest room hasn't had a guest in it for over a year now. Sarah just stays in hotels when she comes to visit and Lucas has been over in wherever, doing his Peace Corps work.

Sydney If you're lonely, I don't know why you don't just go out and get yourself a new girlfriend.

Beverly Right, like I'm going to walk into Charlie's and pick up some hot, young chick looking like this.

Sydney I think you'd be surprised how attractive those girls would find you.

Beverly All I'm saying is that it's not a bad idea for a couple of old dykes to keep each other company.

Sydney What would I do when you have your floozies over for the evening?

Beverly Ha! If I have a floozy over for the evening, you should buy a bottle of champagne and celebrate for all lesbians, everywhere.

Even Sydney cracks a smile.

Beverly (*Referring to the box she's just finished taping and labeling.*) Okay, this one is done. What's next?

Sydney Just those and the tapes. (*She points to a pile of things on the counter.*)

Beverly walks over and looks at the tapes.

Beverly I don't know that I'd have enough to say to fill up all these tapes. I mean, I could tell stories about my clients for years, but I don't know how much I would have to say about myself.

Sydney You'd be surprised. Once you get into the habit, you can't help but get it out this way.

Beverly You're such a quiet thing, though. I never would have guessed you were such a writer.

Sydney My journals have kept me company ever since I left home.

Beverly You better not let anyone else hear you talking about your journals like they're people, they'll have you sent in for an evaluation. Crazy old bat.

Beat.

Beverly Did your son ever read them?

Sydney I caught him once. But I scared him so bad he almost ran away.

Beverly And now you're gonna let all those New York City girls read every last one of them.

Sydney Oh, I don't know that anyone will actually take the time to read them. I don't know how interesting any of it is.

Beverly You don't have to send it, you know.

Sydney I think I'll be glad to be free of some of it. All that searching. All that loss.

Beverly Do you have pictures of them?

Sydney My journals?

Beverly Very funny!

Sydney I have pictures of them around the house. Gio's on my dresser. Ruth is in the living room and dining room. Henry is on the nightstand.

Beverly Will you send any pictures with the journals, of yourself?

Sydney There are a couple pasted in, from Pittsburgh, when I was just starting off. And some of Ruth and I. I let Henry do some drawings in a couple of them when he was younger.

Beverly I really wish you would come and live with me.

Sydney Do you think I'm pitiful? Is that why you want me to move in?

Beverly Because I think we could keep each other company.

Sydney I don't need company.

Beverly You make me sound like a weakling, like I'm foolish for wanting other people around me.

Sydney We're very different, you and I.

Beverly I'm not sure I buy that.

Sydney (*Indicating the packing tape.*) Are you done with that?

Beverly Yes.

Beverly hands Sydney the roll of tape.

Sydney We each have our own way.

Beverly Okay. Have it your way. You certainly don't lack for will.

Sydney Besides, you're young enough to find yourself another lady. You don't need an old wrinkled woman hobbling around your apartment. They'll think I'm your mother.

Beverly I doubt people have much idea what to make of you. You're something quite unique.

Sydney You young liberals always think us old biddies are unique. It's just nostalgia.

Beverly laughs. Sydney cracks a smile.

Scene 20

Volunteer is working at the computer. Sophie is putting things away in the main reading room.

Volunteer You didn't say on this form what the category and subcategories should be.

Sophie On what form?

Volunteer For Sydney Anders' papers.

Sophie walks in from the other room.

Sophie I'll fill that in later.

Volunteer I'm just putting all this in now. Just let me know which keywords to put in, then we can choose a category for it.

Sophie I'm not sure I know where I want it listed yet.

Volunteer Anders—what is that, Dutch? Is she European?

Sophie No, her birth name was Isabella Ricci.

Volunteer Shouldn't we put that in there?

Sophie It's in the notes.

The Volunteer skims the notes.

Volunteer Oh, you're right. Sorry, I haven't gotten to that yet. But the keywords are blank.

Sophie I guess, mother, Wisconsin, World War II…diaries, journals, recordings, poet, Pittsburgh, widow…

Volunteer Didn't someone say she was a recluse? Should we put that in? Or was she a separatist, or something like that?

Sophie No. No, I wouldn't say that. (*Beat.*) Italian-American, married…

Volunteer Do we put that, even though it was illegal?

Sophie They had their own ceremony.

Volunteer Oh, okay. What about closeted, or something like that?

Sophie No, we don't put that on anything.

Volunteer Right, I guess if their stuff is here…

Sophie Working class.

Volunteer You can put that?

Sophie Yes. There aren't a lot of stories like this that people can actually read.

Volunteer Anything else?

Sophie Midwest, Elderly.

Volunteer This is her whole life, though?

Sophie I'm thinking of the things people will search for—the things that will help researchers find her papers. (*Beat.*) Runaway.

Volunteer Really?

Sophie When she was seventeen.

Volunteer Anything else?

Sophie That's all I can think of right now. I'll go back to it later.

Beat.

Volunteer Makes you wonder what keywords they would use for your life if it came here in a bunch of boxes.

Projection

Birds over a wide grassy slope.

Sydney (*Recorded.*) I think part of me would have preferred to remain hidden—to just fade away. Who am I, anyway? What does my life add up to? But I guess I just think of how hard it was for me to find other people like me back then. How hard it was to understand what I was going through. I know it's easier for these girls now, but, I don't know, sometimes you just feel like you look out in the crowd and you can't find anyone like you, you can't find a single friendly face. I suppose these things I'm giving you might end up sitting in boxes for a long time, and maybe no one will ever sit down and read every one, but I like knowing they could, if they wanted to, if they needed to. Someone else struggling to figure it out. I've taken a lot of solace in other people's words over the years. I hope maybe mine can offer that to someone.

Closing

Stagehand enters and turns off the reel-to-reel recorder. She pulls the full reel off the device, pulls a marker out of her pocket and writes something on the reel. Then she finds a box somewhere on a shelf, pulls it down, carefully places the reel inside of it, replaces the box on the shelf, and exits.

End.

Acknowledgements

This play wouldn't exist if the Lesbian Herstory Archives didn't exist, and so I must start by thanking everyone who helped create it, those who have tirelessly worked to maintain it, and everyone who has contributed to its entirely donation-based collection.

Thank you to the members of the Lesbian Herstory Archives' 2011-2012 Lesbian Lives class: Elvis Bakaitis, Gwendolyn Beetham, Maggie Chestnut, Kate Conroy, Nabila Eltantawy, Elfie Knecht, Marya Leonard, Meredith Nelson, Tina Osterhoudt, Ann Pachner, Marie Pascal, Sam Tabet, Elizabeth Tarras, Diane Vreeland, Kerrie Welsh, and Fran Winant. Listening to, laughing with, and learning from each of you helped me not only to see the possibilities for a different kind of learning, but also a different way of viewing the world and being within it. I couldn't be happier that I can now count some of you as friends. Thank you for your ongoing support for this play and the project it gave birth to.

To the Millay Colony, where I was a resident in the fall of 2011 and was able to work in earnest on the first full draft of the play.

To early readers, particularly Amy Caramore.

To Shawn(ta) Smith, whom I came to know through volunteer work and projects at the Archives following the class and with whom a kind of trio has formed with Flavia Rando. More than anything, I believe Shawn and I bonded in our shared love and admiration for Flavia. But I have also come to admire so much about her, not to mention the work she has done and continues to do. Thank you, Shawn.

And the final thanks must go to Flavia Rando. As with others named here, I feel I have learned only a fraction of the things about you, but I cannot say enough how much I appreciate you and the work you have done and continue to do. Your class and your thoughts helped shaped this play primarily because they helped shape me, and for that I can never thank you enough.

About the Author

Alexis Clements is a playwright and journalist based in Brooklyn, NY, where she co-founded the queer writing group and publisher, Private Commission. An alumna of the Women's Project Playwrights Lab, she has been awarded a Dramatists Guild of America fellowship, two Puffin Foundation Artist Grants, a Ludwig Vogelstein Foundation grant, and the Source Theatre's Washington Theatre Festival Literary Prize. Her creative work has been produced and published in both the US and the UK. Selected productions include: *Conversation* (Fringe Festival: Philadelphia, PA); *Enough!* (Highline Park: New York, NY); *Place ReImagined* (Women's Project & River-to-River Festival: New York, NY); *Dance Away Your Debt* (FIGMENT Festival: Governors Island, NY & Dance Parade: New York, NY); *Spitting Against the Wind* (Brooklyn Arts Exchange: Brooklyn, NY & Dixon Place: New York, NY); *Your Own Personal Apocalypse* (One Million Forgotten Moments Project: New York, NY & Chashama: New York, NY); *Causality* (Towngate Theater: Wheeling, WV); and *The Interview* (Edinburgh Fringe Festival: Scotland, UK). She served as a co-editor for the two-volume anthology of plays, *Out of Time & Place*, which includes her performance piece, *Conversation*. Her plays, *Pieces* and *Three Choices*, have been published by *KNOCK*. Her articles, essays, and interviews have appeared in publications such as *Salon*, *Bitch Magazine*, *Autostraddle*, *American Theatre*, *The Brooklyn Rail*, *Two Serious Ladies*, *Nature*, *Frontiers*, and *In the Flesh*. She is a regular contributor, focused on art and performance, to *Hyperallergic*. She has a M.Sc. in Philosophy & History of Science from the London School of Economics and Political Science and a B.A. in Theater Studies from Emerson College.

www.alexisclements.com

TYPEFACE

Typeface: Adobe Caslon [body], Myriad Pro [headings].
Designer: Carol Twombly.

Carol Twombly was born June 13, 1959, in Concord, Massachusetts. She studied at the Rhode Island School of Design and Stanford University. In 1984 Twombly was awarded first prize in the Morisawa Type Competition for her Mirarae typeface. She was the first woman to receive this award for promising typeface designers under the age of 35. Twonbly designed Myriad in the mid-1990s, along with Robert Slimbach, and re-designed Caslon at the same time for Adobe, where she worked for a number of years.

Myriad is a humanist sans-serif typeface best known for its usage by Apple Inc, replacing Apple Garamond as Apple's corporate font since 2002. Myriad is easily distinguished from other sans-serif fonts due to its special "y" descender (tail) and slanting "e" cut.

Caslon is a long-running serif font. First designed by William Caslon in 1722, it was used extensively throughout the British Empire in the early eighteen century, and in the early days of the American Colonies. It was the font used for the US Declaration of Independence, but fell out of favor soon after. It has been revived at various times since then, in particular during the British Arts and Crafts movement and again each time it went through a redesign for technological changes. It continues to be a standard in typography to this day.

OTHER WOMEN TYPEFACE DESIGNERS

Rebecca Alaccari, Jill Bell, Veronika Burian, Kris Holmes, Zuzana Licko, Freda Sack, and Gundrun Zapf von Hesse.

Colophon compiled by Damien Luxe.

You may also enjoy

Private Comissions'
Other Recent Title

Buy your copy today at
privatecommission.wordpress.com

www.ingramcontent.com/pod-product-compliance
Lightning Source LLC
Chambersburg PA
CBHW032148040426
42449CB00005B/442